HAMARTIA / HATCHET

HAMARTIA
HATCHET

Carmen Boullosa

Translated by Lawrence Schimel

WHITE PINE PRESS / BUFFALO, NE YORK

White Pine Press
P.O. Box 236
Buffalo, NY 14201
www.whitepine.org

First published in Spanish under the title *Hamartia (o Hacha)* by Ediciones
Hiperión in co-edition with the Universidad Autónoma de Nueva León,
UANL Republished by permission of the author.

Acknowledgments:
The author & translator give thanks to the editors of the following journals
where some of these poems appeared previously:

Concrete & River: "Crinoline Variations"; *Loch Raven Review:* "The Carrion Fly"
and "The Illusion of Stone." *Latin American Literature Today:* "Axe," "Bermuda Tri-
angle," and "Crinoline Variations"; *Review: Literature and Arts of the Americas,* Issue
99, Volume 52, Number 2, December 2019: "Soup," "The Voice of Death," and
"...What Devours Me When I Don't Write..."

Publication of this book was supported by a grant from the National Endow-
ment for the Arts, which believes that a great nation deserves great art, and with
funds from The Amazon Literary Partnership.

Printed and bound in the United States of America.

ISBN 978-1-945680-39-7

Library of Congress Control Number: 201995798

Hamartia: Error trágico. Defecto. Fallo. Pecado.

Hacha: Vela de cera. Herramienta cortante.

Hamartia: Tragic error. Defect. Flaw. Sin.

Hatchet: Cutting tool.

a Psiche y a Philip Hugues

For Psiche and for Phillip Hughes

Contents

I.

II.

III.

IV.

I.

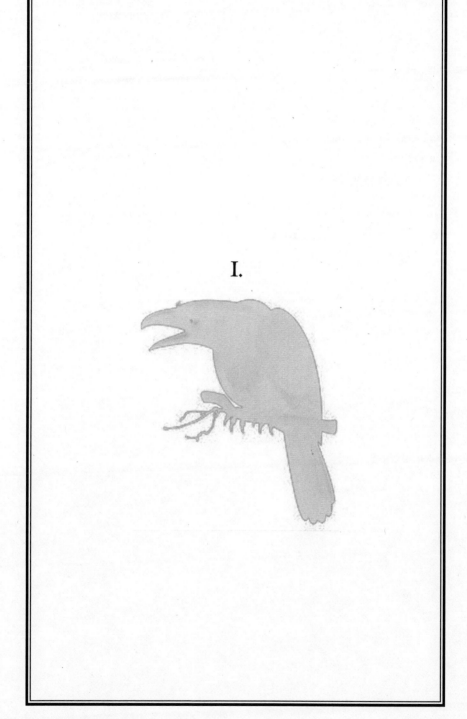

Hacha

Somos hachas de acero y fuego.
Nuestra vida es segar e iluminar.
Con el metal,
nos talamos el tronco.
Con el fuego,
iluminamos el corte,
                    el talar de lo que somos.

Axe

We are hatchets of steel and fire.
We live to reap and illuminate.
With the metal,
we fell the trunk.
With the flame,
we illuminate the cut,
                    the felling of what we are.

Perder, perder

Perdí mi vida a la ruleta.
No fue voluntario.
Soy adicta
al juego,
sólo tenía ese bien
para apostar.

Perdí la vida nomás.
Miraba hacia otro lado
cuando los dados se me escaparon de los dedos.

Los recogió el demonio
antes de yo divisarles la cara.

"Gané la partida",
me dijo.

Entre carcajadas,
sin darle espacio al azar,
me llevó el diablo.

Losing, Losing

I lost my life to the roulette wheel.
It wasn't voluntary.
I'm addicted
to gambling,
had only that left
to bet.

I lost my life, just that.
I was looking the other way
when the dice escaped from my fingers.

The demon gathered them up
before I could see their faces.

"I won,"
he told me.

Cackling,
leaving no room for chance,
the devil seized me.

Estirpe

No fui un robinsoncrusoe,
tampoco mordí la manzana como una eva,
ni perpetré drakoneadas,
ni descubrí los Rayos X que después develarían tus huesos.

No, no participé en asaltos en puertos extranjeros,
no viajé, no exploré, no zozobré en tormentas,
ni descubrí o renové.
Yo no hice nada.

Me echaron del paraíso
sin que lo provocara mi voluntad.

Lineage

I wasn't a robinsoncrusoe,
nor did I bite the apple like some eve,
nor follow in drake's footsteps,
nor discover the x-rays that later revealed your bones.

No, I didn't take part in assaults on foreign ports,
I didn't travel, I didn't explore, I didn't capsize in storms,
I neither discovered nor renewed.
I did nothing at all.

I was expelled from eden
but not of my own accord.

Vejez

Como el pez fuera del agua,
deshidratándose, la piel seca del viejo pierde tensión, se arruga.
Las quijadas quieren desnudarse, repugnándoles el feo vestido.
La calavera anda con prisa por quedar descubierta.

Los viejos no somos como los peces fuera del agua,
porque el pez sin agua muere.
Nuestras vidas no son ríos,
que van a dar a la mar.
Un caudal seco,
el Hombre,
olvidándolo todo,
senil,
regresa a su infancia.

Old Age

Like a fish out of water,
dehydrating, the dry skin of the elderly loses its firmness, it wrinkles.
Jawbones want to undress themselves, disgusted by their ugly covering.
Skulls are in a hurry to be uncovered.

But we elderly are not like fish out of water,
because without water a fish dies.
Our lives are not rivers,
that go to empty into the sea.
A dry riverbed,
mankind,
forgetting everything,
senile,
returns to its childhood.

La voz de la muerte

Voceando la muerte del edificio,
el cuervo (gárgola viva)
negramente grazna:
        "Adiós, Hotel de Dieu,

               ¡adiós!"

En la acera de enfrente,
su coro son los niños; gritan
        "¡Ee!, ¡aa!, ¡iii!".
juegan a las carreras.

Cuando llega el primero a la puerta del Hotel de Dieu,
grazna más alto que los demás, chillando
             "Les gané, ¡gané!,
                ¡perdieron!"
Su aria triunfal pasma la gritería.
Los demás niños dejan de correr.
Giran a ver el vetusto edificio abandonado.
El ganador tose, moqueando.

Sabiéndose triunfante,
          el cuervo
              echa a volar.

The Voice of Death

Giving voice to the building's death,
the crow (live gargoyle)
blackly caws:
> *Adieu, Hotel de Dieu,*
>
> > *adieu!*

On the opposite sidewalk,
its chorus are the children; they shout:
> > *Ee! aa! ii!*

They race one another.

When the first reaches the door of the Hotel de Dieu,
he crows louder than the rest, squawking:
> > *I won! I won!*
> >
> > > *You lost!*

His victorious aria quells their uproar.
The other children cease to run.
They turn to look at the ancient abandoned building.
The winner coughs, nose running.

Knowing itself triumphant,
> the crow
>
> > takes flight.

Microondas

En la charola giratoria del horno
descanso la bolsa de papel
cargada de dormidas semillas de maíz.

Cierro la puerta.
Presiono el botón pidiéndole tres minutos.
Empieza el canto del microondas.
Quiero oír en él, como en el del pájaro, algún mensaje de los dioses.

En su oscura puerta reflejante
—remedo industrial del espejo de obsidiana—,
aparecen mis hijos.

El microondas desprende a la materia del lazo natural del tiempo.
En su espejo (en su puerta), estoy con mis dos hijos recién nacidos, en brazos.
Se filtra su calor,
nos funde a los tres en una sola imagen.

Aparece la luz, la luz del Valle de México.
Las flores de la jacaranda
caen.
En el horno, el tiempo corre en desorden.
Las semillas de maíz bailan,
ríen pequeños estallidos,
y mis dos bebes empiezan a gatear.

Entre un segundo y otro,
antes de lo que digo una sílaba
—repiquetean los maicitos—,
los pequeños dan sus primeros pasos
(la niña en el piso de madera,
Juan en el patio de casa),
castañetean las campanadas del maíz bailaor.

Microwave

Upon the oven's rotating tray
I set the paper bag
full of sleeping kernels of corn.

I shut the door,
press the button for three minutes.
The microwave's song begins.
I want to hear in it, like in birdsong, some message from the gods.

In its dark reflective door
(industrial imitation of the obsidian mirror),
my children appear.

The microwave removes matter from the natural bond of time.
In its mirror (in its door), I hold my two newborn children in my arms.
Its heat filters out,
melts us three into a single image.

The light comes on, the light of the Valle de México.
The jacaranda blossoms
fall.
In the oven, time scrambles forward.
The kernels of corn dance,
small bursts of laughter,
and my two babies begin to crawl.

Between one second and the next,
before I can say a syllable
(the tiny kernels drumming),
my little ones take their first steps
(the girl on the wooden floor,
Juan in the yard),
the ring and clatter of the dancing corn.

El horno anuncia otro de sus segundos:
los dos niños aprenden a ir solos al baño,
están en la escuela,
salen a bailar
—son maracas los maíces, panderos, timbales—.

Atrás del zumbar mecánico del horno,
oigo a los chicos reír.
Golpean los platillos las rosetas de maíz,
estruendo, estruendo:
jóvenes los dos hijos, viven conmigo en Nueva York.

El horno se detiene.
Un chasquito, dos, las palomitas se detienen a pensar:
silencio.
Silencio distinto al de la flor de jacaranda cuando besa el asfalto,
silencio sin frescura, sin color.
Silencio que no recuerda el baile,
ni el repiqueteo, los metales o las percusiones,
o a los tacones golpeando adentro del horno devenido en tablado y cas-
tañuela.
En tres minutos se consumieron dos infancias.

Silencio:
abro la puerta del horno,
su luz (de minúsculo quirófano en hospital depauperado)
pega en mi pecho, en mi corazón desnudo.

Desgarro la bolsa de papel.
Exhala una bocanada de vapor en la que veo a mis hijos,
en dos horas distintas,
en dos aeropuertos diferentes,
tomar el avión de vuelta a México.
Mis hijos se van, ya no vivirán conmigo, nunca.

The oven counts down another of its seconds:
the two children learn to go to the bathroom alone,
they are at school,
they go out and dance
(the corn kernels are maracas, tambourines, kettledrums).

Above the oven's mechanical buzz,
I hear my children's laughter.
The corn rosettes beat upon the dish,
bang, bang:
teens now, my two children live with me in New York.

The oven stops.
A clack, a second, the popcorn stops to think:
silence.
Silence nothing like the jacaranda blossom when it kisses the asphalt,
silence that's stale, colorless.

Silence that doesn't remember the dance,
the drumming, the horns or the percussions,
the heels pounding inside the oven transformed into dancefloor and castanets.
In three minutes two childhoods were consumed.

Silence:
I open the oven's door,
its light (like that of a minuscule surgery in some impoverished hospital)
hits my chest, my naked heart.

I tear open the paper bag.
It exhales a gust of steam in which I see my children,
in two different times,
in two different airports,
catching a flight back to Mexico.
My children leave, they'll no longer live with me, ever again.

La fresca jacaranda pisoteada,
el suelo tinto de morada, escarnecida luz.

El reloj regresa a su cordura.
Vacío la bolsa.
Saltan las semillas en sus nuevos vestidos blancos almidonados,
caen al amplio platón,
una fúnebre, pálida reminiscencias de la cuaresma.
Ignorándola, las palomitas crujen como si fueran hechas de seda.

En cada semilla hay abierta una flor
de pétalos secos, crocantes.
En cada palomita,
el juego del niño, las horas frente al pupitre,
la escapada adolescente, sus fiestas,
acicalarse para salir a buscar trabajo.

Se me escapan tres lágrimas.
Al caer,
marchitan alguna de las flores de maíz
apagándoles su ilusión de seda nueva,
ahogándoles el baile, dejándolas
como a aquella flor de jacaranda,
cuando el viento, tentado por su palidez encendida,
acarició a la viuda de un árbol vivo,
como restan los padres,
viudos siempre de la infancia de sus hijos.

The fresh jacaranda trod upon,
the ground dyed purple, the light mocked.

The clock returns to its senses.
I empty the bag.
The seeds in their new starched white dresses leap,
they fall onto the broad plate,
like a covering veil, evoking Lent.
Unaware of this, the popcorn rustles as if made from silk.

In each seed there is an open flower
of dry, crunchy petals.
In each piece,
a child's game, hours spent at a school desk,
a teen escapade, their parties,
getting dressed up to hunt for jobs.

Three tears escape.
Falling,
they make some of the corn flowers wilt,
quenching their excitement of new silk,
drowning the dance, leaving them
like that jacaranda blossom,
when the wind, tempted by its fiery paleness,
caressed that widow from a living tree,
as parents are removed,
forever widowed from our children's childhoods.

El partido

En la cancha,
Piermario Morosini
de uniforme rojo,
la mirada fija en el balón.

Cerca de él está la ansiada meta, la portería, la red,
la Gloria.

Sólo para Piermario,
se escenifica un milagro:
el mundo trepida.
La Tierra es una pelota en vuelo dislocado.
La iluminada bóveda celeste,
también, un tiro disparado.
El cosmos tambalea, los giros planetarios brincan.

Trastabilla Piermario Morosini.
Sube la mano derecha al pecho.
Se le doblan las rodillas.

Un corto zumbido intenso,
espetado al oído de Piermario,
parodiando un excitado ¡goooool!,
anticipa el silencio más perfecto.

Piermario cae.

"Un súbito malestar", dice la locutora que describe la escena.
Sus palabras no siguen la escena:
los músculos desobedecen sin tensión al futbolista,
no perciben el balón,
no reconocen el pasto,
el sol, el aire tibio, los espectadores,
la agitación, ni su propia inmovilidad.

The Match

On the pitch,
Piermario Morosini
in his red uniform,
gaze fixed on the ball.

Near him is the longed-for target, the goal, the net,
Glory.

For Piermario alone,
a miracle is staged:
the world shakes.
Earth is a ball in disjointed flight.
The illuminated celestial sphere
is a sudden shot.
The cosmos trembles, the planetary spins jerk.

Piermario Morosini stumbles.
His right hand rises to his chest.
His knees fold.

A short intense buzz,
spat into Piermario's ear,
parodying an excited "gooooooal!,"
anticipates the most perfect silence.

Piermario falls.

"A sudden collapse," says the announcer describing the scene.
Her words don't follow the action:
the player's muscles disobey, nerveless,
they don't perceive the ball,
they don't recognize the pitch,
the sun, the warm air, the crowd,
the uproar, not even their own immobility.

En un asiento del estadio,
la cerveza rubia del vaso brillante al sol,
se paraliza,
rima con el corazón de Piermario.
Sin espuma,
ya no burbujea.

En la cancha, reposa la pelota,
imitando al corazón de Piermario.

El verde pasto y la bóveda celeste quedan en suspenso,
estática fotografía amateur
de la sangre y los pulmones del futbolista.

Lo encamillan,
le ajustan la mascarilla de oxígeno,
y sobreviene un segundo movimiento:
en vilo, Piermario Morosini,
inerte, sin pálpito,
es un objeto sin vuelo,
lo llevan de mano en mano.

Es un bulto,
desinflado.

Nadie lanza el pase formidable,
tampoco hay portero.
Deslizan a Piermario adentro de la ambulancia,
lo enfundan como a un mensaje escrito en un sobre usado.

El caucho de los neumáticos roza el pavimento.
La grabación de la sirena va cantando
un breve, repetitivo, colombino u-u-u empalagoso.

In a seat in the stadium,
the pale beer of a glass shines in the sun,
stock still,
rhymes with Piermario's heart.
Foamless,
no longer bubbling.

On the pitch, the ball rests,
imitating Piermario's heart.

The green pitch and the celestial sphere are suspended,
static amateur photograph
of the soccer player's blood and lungs.

He's put on a stretcher,
they adjust his oxygen mask,
and a second movement takes place:
in the air, Piermario Morosini,
inert, unbeating,
is a flightless object,
carried from hand to hand.

He is a bundle,
disinflated.

Nobody makes that tremendous pass,
there is no goalie.
They slide Piermario into the ambulance,
wrap him up like a message written on a used envelope.

The rubber of the tires rubs the pavement.
The recorded siren sings
a brief, repetetive, cloying ululation: u-u-u.

Los neumáticos frenan en seco.

Acarreándola, bruscos extraen la camilla de Piermario,
como si jugaran fut americano.
Con un pase brusco,
métenlo al hospital de Pescara.

Apenas trasponer la entrada, el jugador muere.

¡Ay!
Confiando en el poder de la monosílaba
que reta (o evoca) a Dios,
Piermario hubiera querido morir como un piermario,
en acción,
en la cancha,
jugando en la Selección Nacional de futbol.

Como querríamos morir nosotros:
                            la cancha por sepulcro.

The tires brake abruptly.

Rough hands extract Piermario's gurney, lugging him
as if they were playing football.
With a brusque pass, like scoring,
they push him into the Pescara hospital.

Just through the door, the player dies.

Oh!
Trusting in the power of the monosyllable
that challenges (or evokes) God,
this is how Piermario would have wished to die,
in action,
on the field,
playing in the soccer National Selection.

As we'd all like to die:
                                with the pitch for our tomb.

...eso que me devora cuando no escribo...

Escribí huyéndole.
Me tocó una vez, y en la mudez me dejó
      eso que me devora cuando no escribo.

Fui de una novela a otra,
de un poema
me arrojé,
      como el loco al precipicio,
            al siguiente.

Me detuve
      y me miró a los ojos:
           eso que me devora si no escribo.

...What Devours Me When I Don't Write...

I wrote, fleeing from it.
It touched me once, and left me mute,
        what devours me when I don't write.

I went from one novel to the next,
from one poem
I threw myself,
            like a madman from the cliff,
                            to the next.

I paused
        and it stared me in the eyes:
                        what devours me when I don't write.

Lluvia seca

Lluvia de flores en Brooklyn.
    Caen minúsculos pétalos blancos
    anunciándonos
    la primavera,
        nos bañan
       sin agua
           en frescas
              risas hipotéticas.

Dry Rain

Rain of flowers in Brooklyn.
      Minute white petals fall
      heralding
      the spring,
          bathing us
          without water
              in fresh
                  hypothetical laughter.

La sopa

Esa sopa
con avellanas tostadas
es un poema escrito en Clermont.

Leyéndolo,
me lo comí
sin saberlo descifrar.

Efímero sopapoema,
irrepetible en otra ciudad,
no pide sino el recuerdo para leerlo una vez más:
es mi infancia
renovada,
esta sopa de avellana es la vida de cuando yo tenía tres años.
No la tendré ya más.

Soup

This soup
with toasted hazelnuts
is a poem written in Clermont.

Reading it,
I ate it up
without knowing how to decipher it.

Ephemeral soupoem,
unrepeatable in another city,
asking for nothing but that memory to read it once more:
  it is my childhood
   renewed,
this hazelnut soup is my life when I was three years old.
I won't have it ever again.

Dos deseos

Dos deseos intensos,
paralelos, rieles
bien aparejados:
comer delicias
y
morir para siempre.

¿Se contradicen entre ellos?
Devoro
y me dejo devorar por los años,
humano al fin.

Two Desires

Two intense desires,
in parallel, rails
well-harnessed:
to eat delicacies
and
die once and for all.

Do they contradict one another?
I devour
and let myself be devoured by the years,
human at last.

La casa del Amor

Viví la infancia en la casa del Amor.
Desconocí las mordidas del fuego.

Pero desde los quince,
quedé orillada a saltar sobre la hoguera.
Por inercia,
creí que la cruzaría sin riesgo.

Soy lo que come la flama,
lo que asfixia el humo,
lo que ilumina
ansiosa la combustión,

No soy cenizas.
El fuego, que me ha herido,
se aviva al morderme
dejándome dolor punzante en el nervio.
En lo que resta de carne queda la fealdad de la quemadura.
En la memoria, el hueso intacto de la casa indestructible del Amor.

Soy una cifra más
para la cuenta final del Gran Todo,
fragmento, pedazo, *cadavra* móvil, *fuegaguí*,
      —y soy, iluminada, la memoria intacta,
        la indevorable viva.

The House of Love

I lived my childhood in the house of Love.
I never knew the bite of the fire.

But since I was fifteen, I was backed into a corner
after leaping over the bonfire.
Out of inertia,
I thought I could cross it without risk.

I am what the flame devours,
what the smoke chokes,
what combustion
anxiously illuminates.

I am not ash.
The fire, which has wounded me,
revives as it bites into me
leaving a piercing pain along the nerve.
In the surviving flesh, the ugliness of the burn remains.
In my memory, the intact bone of the indestructible house of Love.

I am one more number
for the final count of the Great Everything,
fragment, chunk, moving *cadavra, fuegafui*—
            and, enlightened, I am intact memory,
                    undevourable life.

En la sala

En la sala de palacio
donde Molière actuó por primera vez para un rey,
las Cariátides se burlan
como entonces
fingiendo solemne seriedad.

In the Room

In the room of the palace
where Molière first acted for a king,
the Caryatids mock
as they did then,
feigning a solemn seriousness.

Napoleón actor

El actor tiene cara de Napoleón;
le dieron el papel protagónico porque es su calca,
pero cada gesto, cada movimiento suyos
deshacen el notable parecido.
Este mequetrefe no es Bonaparte.

Repite al dedillo las frases del emperador,
con buena voz.
Con el porte,
el alto, los hombros y el gesto del grande,
responde con asustados reflejos de perro faldero,
de roedor nervioso.

El espíritu se resiste a toda forma.
La apariencia es burbuja.
La materia se escapa con el alma.

Enacting Napolean

The actor looks just like Napoleon;
they gave him the leading role because he could be his clone,
but every gesture, every move he makes
undoes that notable likeness.
This good-for-nothing is no Bonaparte.

He repeats the emperor's phrases by heart,
with a good voice.
With the same bearing,
the height, shoulders and gestures of that great man,
he responds with the frightened reflexes of a lapdog,
of a nervous rodent.

The spirit resists in every way.
Appearance is a bubble.
Matter escapes with the soul.

Lanzas

¿Cuántas veces he visitado tus lanzas, Ucello?
Hace cuarenta años,
crucé la mirada con uno de los de a pie.
Él caminaba hacia el frente de batalla,
lo vi carne de cañón,
lo di por muerto.
Me creí intocable.

Hoy frente a tus lanzas, Ucello,
comprendo que él es cauteloso.
Nos reconocemos.
Sus ojos me despiden
con su caminar perpetuo.
Sabe que soy yo quien va de salida,
yo la efímera.

El de pie y yo somos pares.
Tampoco hubo gloria en mi destino.
No cargué el banderín,
no anduve a caballo, no llevé el mando.
Me apagué como el hacha
al terminar su cera y agotar el cabo.
Aquí dejo la última chispa.

Spears

How many times have I seen your spears, Ucello?
Forty years ago,
I crossed glances with one of the standing men.
He walked toward the battlefront,
I saw him cannon fodder,
I gave him up for dead.
I believed myself untouchable.

Today, facing your spears, Ucello,
I understand that he is cautious.
We recognize one another.
His eyes bid me farewell
with his perpetual walking.
He knows that I am the one who is exiting,
I the ephemeral

That standing man and I are a pair.
There was no glory in my fate either.
I bore no standard,
I didn't ride on horseback, didn't lead the charge.
I was snuffed out like a tall candle
when its wax is gone and the wick consumed.
This is where I leave the final spark.

Nariz

No me hagas esto, nariz.
Donde quieras, manifiesta tus alergias,
pero no te perdono hacer el teatro aquí.

Fuiste mi olfato,
el adelantado conquistador,
contigo intuí.
Ahora eres el llanto de un capricho ajeno
por el que debo dar la cara,
el enemigo en casa.

Fuiste arrogante,
hoy te arrodillas perpetua ante el pañuelo.

Subida en mí,
me recuerdas
que crucé la vida viajando en nave ajena.

Mis ojos alimentarán los pájaros que no serán cuervos que yo no crié,
y la mirada será una desaparecida insepulta.

Nose

Don't do this to me, nose.
Unleash your allergies wherever you want,
but I won't forgive your putting on this show here.

You were my instinct,
the forward conqueror,
with you I intuited.
Now you are the wail of a distant whim
for which I must show my face,
the enemy within.

You were arrogant,
now you kneel everlasting before the handkerchief.

Prevailing,
you remind me
that I crossed life journeying on a foreign ship.

My eyes will feed crows I never saw,
my gaze—a woman, disappeared and unburied.

Barriga

Barriguita de mi ser querido,
no crezcas más.
Dicen que acortas la longevidad.
No me importas por ti,
sino por lo que sospecho que alimentas.
Eres caníbal. Comes hombres.
Vete.

Belly

Oh beer belly of my beloved,
don't grow any more
They say you shorten our lifespan.
It's not you yourself that worries me,
but what I suspect you feed on.
You are a cannibal. You devour men.
Get out of here!

Vagabundo

El vagabundo finge leer en el subway.
Dormita y vigila sus bolsas mientras lo pretende.
El aire que entra cuando se abren las puertas del vagón,
pasa las hojas de su libro,
adelante y atrás,
hacia atrás y adelante.

Con el vagabundo,
el libro finge,
dormita
y
vigila.

Tramp

The tramp pretends to read on the subway.
He drowses and keeps guard over his bags as he does so.
The air that enters when the doors open
turn the pages of his book,
forward and back,
back and forward.

With the tramp,
the book pretends,
drowses
and
keeps watch.

Niño en el metro

No trae zapatos, el niño.
Se acuclilla junto a la puerta para que no lo vean los guardias.
Escena nueva en mi ciudad.

¿No me ve,

o yo no lo había visto antes?
Mis zapatos rechinan de vergüenza.
Se esconde tras la puerta, bajo el asiento.
Juega saltando entre una estación y otra.
No mendiga.
Le basta
para comer
el bofetón que es su presencia.

Child in the Metro

He is not wearing shoes, this child.
He crouches by the door so the guards won't see him.
A new scenario in my city.

Does he not see me,

or did I not see him before?
My shoes squeak with shame.
He hides behind the door, beneath the seat.
He plays at jumping between one station and another.
He doesn't beg.
For him to eat
the hard slap of his mere presence
is enough.

El Tren

Corren,
dejando atrás
al tren,
los árboles
pelones;

corren,
los brazos en alto,
desnudos,
en masa;

corren,
desnudos;
corren, asustados,
y no llegan
a ningún lado.

La vida nunca fue un río
—¡está pelona!—:
      nos va dejando atrás
      como al tren
      sus árboles.

The Train

They run,
leaving behind
the train,
the bare
trees;

they run,
their arms held high,
naked,
in a mob;

they run,
naked;
they run, frightened,
and never get
anywhere.

Life was never a river
(it's harsh):
       it leaves us behind
       as the train does
       with its trees.

La mosca panteonera

Entra rompiendo plaza
la enorme mosca panteonera.
Negra, voraz,
eléctrica.

Cruza por la ventana abierta.
Reclama todo el territorio.
Virtuosa zumba y vuela en círculos,
danzas
a pie de aire.

Incansable, interrumpe
mi prevista siesta.
Hace piruetas sobre las blancas sábanas,
me espanta el descanso.

Dejo la cama,
derrotada por su agitación.

Ella regresa a la ventana
y en su marco
—la que ganó el apodo de Panteonera
a punta de sobrevolar cadáveres humanos y animales,
desafiando al llanto, al rito del funeral,
al apetito de la hiena
y su manjar de carne corrupta
manducando fresca la carne del rastro en banquetes sangrientos—,
la mosca se desploma,
cae
patas arriba.

Los muertos regresan, tranquilos, a la tierra.

The Carrion Fly

The enormous carrion fly
enters the fray.
Black, ravenous,
electric.

It crosses through the open window.
Stakes claim to the entire territory.
Virtuous buzz and flight in circles
dancing
on tip toe in the air.

Tireless, it interrupts
my planned siesta.
It pirouettes above the white sheets,
shooing away my rest.

I get out of bed,
defeated by its movement.

The fly returns to the window
and in its frame—
having earned the nickname Carrion
from flying over the corpses of humans and animal,
defying grief, funeral rites,
the the hyena's appetite
and its meal of rotting flesh
gorging on the meat right from its jaws in bloody banquets—
it collapses,
falls
feet up in the air.

The dead return, calm, to earth.

Temo las maldiciones,
los embrujos,
las letanías
que sobre este acto escupirán
los profetas y la adivinadora que en la esquina de casa lee la suerte, si le
das diez pesos.

El silencio no es oro: es ella.
Veo la mosca, temblando como la hoja vieja.

La mosca se agita, se reincorpora,
zumba de nuevo,
otra vez la panteonera.

Su cuerpo danza en espantoso contoneo,
en diminutos saltos y volutas mareadas.
Vuela un tramito,
y cae otra vez,
patas arriba.
Parece (de nuevo) muerta.

¡Doble cadáver pesará en mi destino!

Cierro la ventana.
Dejo la habitación,
e intento hacer oídos sordos al zumbido que (por tercera vez) recomienza.
¿Por qué,
mosca?
¿Por qué motivo me haces esto?
¿Qué tengo yo que te atrae?
¿Por qué elegiste el momento de mi siesta,
mis sábanas limpias, los botones recién abiertos en el florero?
¿Qué tengo yo para darte?

I fear the curses,
the damnations,
the litanies
that will be spat over this act
by the prophets and the fortune teller on the corner who reads fortunes
for 10 pesos.

The silence is not golden: the fly is.
I see it, trembling like a dried leaf.

The fly twitches, gets up,
buzzes again,
the gravedigger once more.

Its body dances in a fearful swaying,
in miniature leaps and dizzy spirals.
It flies for a bit,
and falls again,
feet in the air.
It seems (once again) dead.

A double cadaver will weigh on my fate!

I close the window.
I leave the room,
and try to be deaf to the buzzing that (for a third time) begins anew.
Why,
fly?
Why are you doing this to me?
What do I have that attracts you?
Why did you choose this moment of my siesta,
my clean sheets, the recently-opened buds in the vase?
What do I have to give you?

¿Me has escogido a mí
para representarte Lázara negra?

¿Es por mí que resucitas?
¿Soy yo la carne que buscas?
¿Vienes en mí a morir?
¿O sólo soy un testigo azaroso,
un tropiezo, un error,
yo la carne para esta Lázara infausta, negra?

Have you chosen me
to play your black Lazarus?

Is it for me you've come back to life?
Am I the flesh you're looking for?
Am I your final resting place?
Or am I just a random witness,
a stumble, a mistake,
I the flesh for this ill-fated, black Lazarus?

Estrella muerta

La estrella muerta
sin embargo se mueve.
Su corazón palpita,
devórase devorándonos en su nueva oscuridad magnética.
Ya no tiene masa,
es el peso del final,
en gerundio se expande.
Implosionará, simultánea se comerá y se expulsará.

Bajo su luz
—rojiza, oscura
mi corazón palpita
en su influencia.

Dead Star

The dead star
nonetheless moves.
Its heart beats,
devouring itself devouring us in its new magnetic darkness.
It no longer has mass,
it is the weight of the end,
expanding infinitely.
It will implode, simultaneously devouring and expelling itself.

Beneath its light—
reddish, dark
my heart beats
to its influence.

La ilusión de la piedra

Eternas son la piedra y el árbol,
a nuestros ojos.

Los años pasan,
el hombre envejece,
la piedra no se altera,
las hojas, en un baile anual, se renuevan.

Frágil y sorda es la vista del homínido:
el castaño morirá y la piedra será polvo.
Sólo aquello que huye permanece,
sólo restará el recuerdo de la fuga.

La memoria
—como el barro—
                              no se irá.

The Illusion of the Stone

Eternal are the stone and the tree
to our eyes.

Years pass,
men age,
but stone doesn't change,
leaves, in an annual dance, are renewed.

Fragile and deaf is the hominid's vision:
the chestnut tree will die and the stone become dust.
Only that which flees endures,
only the remembrance of the flight will remain.

Memory
(like mud)
             will endure.

Todo se rompe

Todo, todo se rompe:
la mariposa vuela tras troncharse la rama,
yo la había visto, otra hoja amarilla.
No es muerte, me dirán, su papaloteo gracioso.
Verla me hiela la sangre.
Yo soy otra rama inmóvil, porque la que fuera hoja es mariposa y vuela.
Todo, todo se rompe.

En la palma de mi mano cae la espora volantina,
blanca y temblorosa,
pálida como un remedo de brisa.
Todo, todo se rompe.
No es muerte, me dirán
tosiendo los asmáticos alérgicos,
no es muerte nuestra muerte, es vuestra vida.

Todo, todo se rompe.
El hermoso libro, sólido, bello.
Lo abro, las hojas quedan viudas unas de otras,
las líneas rompen otra vez a Karenina contra las vías.

Rama dije quedar, por ver volar la mariposa.
Todo, todo se rompe,
y así yo —es la vida— sobre el río sin el árbol,
las vidas van a dar a la mar.

Everything Breaks

Everything, everything breaks:
the butterfly flies after the branch snaps,
I had seen it, another yellow leaf.
It is not death, they will tell me, its funny last gasps.
Seeing it freezes my blood.
I'm another unmoving branch, for what was leaf is butterfly and flies away.
Everything, everything breaks.

Into the palm of my hand falls the unanchored spore,
white and trembling,
pale as a parody of breeze.
Everything, everything breaks.
It is not death, the allergic asthmatics
will tell me coughing,
our death is not death, it is your life.

Everything, everything breaks.
The beautiful book, solid, lovely.
I open it, the pages become widowed one from the others,
the lines once again break Karenina against the tracks.

Branch said: stay, to see the butterfly's flight.
Everything, everything breaks,
and so will I (that's life) above the treeless river,
our lives will flow into the sea.

El vino

El cordero sacrificial no murió,
se bebió su propia sangre,
pobrecito,
pero con tres sorbos, sobrevivió.

El vino de sus verdugos también llegó para quedarse.

The Wine

The sacrificial lamb didn't die,
it drank of its own blood,
poor thing,
but with just three sips, it survived.

The wine of its executioners also came to stay.

Los árboles

Los árboles
aplauden el paso del viento
con sus hojas
inocentes
festejando
sin saber
el signo
de la tormenta.

Cobijan con sus hojas
y mecen con sus ramas
a la tarde fresca,
amparándonos del esperpento

medio instante nada más, porque
nada puede contra el parpadeo de la tarde.
Oscurece por completo el día,
amenaza,
incendiando un momento el cielo.
Asfixia el baile de las hojas:

caen con el golpe diurno del poder de la noche.
Sobre el piso,
ahogadas entre los charcos de la copiosa lluvia,
ya no inocentes,
hipócritas fingen dormir.

The Trees

The trees
applaud the passing of the wind
with their leaves
innocently
celebrating
unknowingly
the sign
of the storm.

They shelter with their leaves
and rock in their branches
the fresh afternoon,
shielding it from the grotesque

half a moment nothing more, because
nothing can stand against the afternoon's blinking.
The day darkens completely,
threatening,
firing the sky for a moment.
The dance of the leaves chokes:

they fall beneath this diurnal blow of the power of night.
On the floor,
drowned among the puddles of the copious rain,
no longer innocent,
the hypocrites feign sleep.

El Puy de Dôme

Fuiste, volcán Puy de Dôme,
el oído de los dioses.

Los peregrinos galos
te ofrendaron ex votos.
De la mano de los divinos lloviste buenaventuras.

La edad te fue dejando sordo.
Viejos como tú, los dioses
olvidaron también que existían los hombres.

Pero tu piel siguió igual, juvenil cada verano, y estás de pie,
llevas cada amanecer un nuevo vestido,
cada atardecer tu infancia perpetua.

En cambio los dioses... en su lecho noche y día,
desaliñados pasan los días sin distinguir la hora.
De ellos, mejor ni hablar.

The Puy de Dôme

You, volcano Puy de Dôme, were
the ear of the gods.

Gallic pilgrims
offer you ex-votos.
From the hand of the divine you rained good fortune.

Age left you deaf.
Old like you, the gods
also forgot the existence of men.

But your skin remains the same, youthful each summer, and you're stand-
ing,
you wear a new dress each dawn,
every afternoon your perpetual childhood.

The gods, on the other hand... in their bed night and day,
listlessly while away their days without noting the time.
Of them, it's better not to speak.

II.

Cruzando la cordillera en tren

El cielo se cayó al piso.
Por eso llora sin consuelo el monte,
delgadas cascadas ruedan por sus faldillas.

El espantapájaros también cayó del árbol.
La rama lo detiene al vuelo
                              de un brazo.

Crossing the Mountains by Train

The sky fell to the ground.
That's why the mountain weeps inconsolably,
slender cascades rolling down its skirts.

The scarecrow also fell from the tree.
A branch breaks its flight
                              by an arm.

Los rieles
en la orilla del precipicio
sienten la tentación de arrojarse al vacío.
Lento el tren,
entre lloronas cascadas
y el cielo resbaladizo,
los sujeta con pinzas a sus túneles
y con un broche al somnoliento Chamborigaud
antes de que salgan volando.

Sube el tren a Genolhac,
cierro el pico de vértigo
a mi costado picos nevados,
pelones, calvos de lo viejos.

The tracks
on the cliff's edge
feel tempted to throw themselves into the void.
Slowly the train,
between crying waterfalls
and the slippery sky,
pins them to their tunnels
clasps them to the sleepy Chamborigaud
before they fly off.

The train climbs up to Genolhac,
I close my mouth in vertigo,
at my side snow-covered peaks,
bare and bald from old age.

En Villefort,
el tren,
menos agarrado de sus uñas.

Pisando nubes,
en Grand Combe-La Pise:
      "agachen la cabeza, pasajeros,
      si no se rasparían la frente
      con el manto del cielo";
            "recójanse las faldas, señoras,
            o las nubes humedecerían sus dobladillos".

In Villefort,
the train
no longer clings so tightly by its nails.

Treading on clouds,
in Grand Combe-La Pise:
      lower your heads, passengers,
      or you'll scrape your foreheads
      against the mantle of the sky";
            "gather your skirts, ladies,
            or the clouds will dampen their hems."

Nieve, nieve.
Llegamos sin desearlo a la cima.

Más alto aún, en Bastide de Saint Laurent,
la nieve barniza todas las ramas de todos los árboles,
artificialmente minuciosa.

Snow, snow.
Without wishing to, we arrive at the top.

Even higher, in Bastide de Saint Laurent,
snow varnishes all the branches of all the leaves,
artificially meticulous.

Empezamos la bajada, Chapeauroux,
escarpados peñascos de zapatos de agua.

Alleyras,
el otoño es aquí perpetuo y tras él
rocas inmensas hablan las lenguas de los antiguos dioses.

We begin the descent, Chapeauroux,
steep crags with shoes of water.

Alleyras,
autumn is eternal here and beyond it
immense rocks speak the languages of the ancient gods.

Langeac, el río se va con lo suyo a otra parte,
las montañas se alejan también,
copetean al fondo de nieve.
Otra vez se sabe que aquí gobiernan los hombres.
Quedamos una vez más a solas.
El cielo ha quedado lejos,
nos quedamos
sin los dioses,
desamparados,
hoscos adanes y evas, urgidos de techo, hambrientos de comida.

Langeac, the river leaves with its things for elsewhere,
the mountains also draw away,
cresting the backdrop with snow.
Again one understands that men rule here.
We are alone once more.
The sky has remained distant,
we remain
godless,
defenceless,
sullen adams and eves, urgently in need of shelter, hungry for food.

III.

Variaciones de miriñaque

Todo corre
                (el pez, la hormiga)
y yo hacia la tumba,
                      último miriñaque.

Corro, del hilván y la gramática de mis vestidos
                —gran miriñaque—,
a la risa dibujada en la calavera del muerto.
...

Crinoline Variations

Everything rushes
         (the fish, the ant)
and I toward the tomb,
         my final crinoline.

I run, from the basting and the grammar of my dresses
         (great crinoline),
toward the laughter drawn on the dead man's skull.
...

"Adiós" —sus últimas palabras—, "¡muera el gobierno del miriñaque!"

Voy a bordo de mi tumba,
          por la vida en miriñaque.

"Goodbye," her final words. "Death to the power of the crinoline!"

I travel aboard my tomb,

                    in a crinoline my entire life.

"Calladito",
dijo el pez,
"voy que vuelo en miriñaque".

Viajó y viajó,
la ballena;
el mar fue su miriñaque.

"Hush,"
said the fish,
"I'm out of here in a crinoline."

It journeyed and journeyed,
the whale;
the sea was its crinoline.

Todo corre,
y yo a mi tumba
a quitarme el miriñaque.

Del gobierno del miriñaque,
me sacan un remo
                    y un chocolate.

Everything rushes,
and I to my tomb
to take off my crinoline.

From the governance of the crinoline,
they take from me an oar
                    and a chocolate.

IV.

Triángulo de las Bermudas

I.
Un pantalón tras otro —ahora puedo llamarlos por su nombre trisílabo—:
fueron invitación al Triángulo de las Bermudas.

Navegué; me extravié en sus aguas imposibles; naufragué.
Sobreviví encallando en una isla desierta, el pantalón (uno
tras otro) hecho andrajos
y muy lejos de mí.

Bermuda Triangle

I.
One pair after another (now I can call them by their trisyllable name)
were an invitation to the Bermuda Triangle.

I sailed; I lost myself in impossible waters; I capsized.
I survived, running aground on a desert island, my clothes (one pair
after another) becoming tatters
far removed from me.

2.
Se pinta el triángulo
en las faldillas
de mi corazón.

En las faldillas
de mi corazón
me pierdo
irremediablemente.

3.
Me sostengo en el cuerpo firme de mi marido,
pero sigue hundiéndoseme el corazón,
en la campaña perpetua del Triángulo dicho,
decidido a devorarme.
Me basta saberlo presente para perder toda calma.
Zozobro. No me pierdo. No encallaré. Resistiré.
Sabré ser un pez fuera del agua.

2.
The triangle is drawn
on the skirts
of my heart.

In the skirts
of my heart
I lose myself
irredeemably.

3.
I am buoyed by my husband's solid body,
but my heart keeps sinking,
in the aforementioned Triangle's perpetual campaign
I decide to devour myself.
It's enough for me to know it's there to lose all calm
I flounder. I don't lose myself. I won't run aground. I shall resist.
I'll learn to be a fish out of water.

The Author

Carmen Boullosa is the author of a dozen volumes of poetry, the most recent ones, *Hamartia* (Hiperión, Madrid), *La patria insomne* (Hiperión, Madrid) and *La impropia* (Taller Martín Pescador, Michoacán, México). One of her poems ("Angel Sound - Mexico City") was published in the *American Poetry Review* in 2013. She has also published eighteen novels. The most recent, *El libro de Ana / The Book of Ana*, was published by Coffee House Press in 2020. Her preceding book, *Texas: The Great Theft*, was shortlisted for the PEN Translation Prize). She has also published two books of essays, and ten plays (seven staged). Her work has been published by leading houses in Latin America and Spain and translated into ten languages.

The Translator

Lawrence Schimel writes in both Spanish and English and has published over one hundred books in many different genres—including fiction, poetry, non-fiction, and comics—and for both children and adults.

He has published two poetry chapbooks written in English: *Fairy Tales for Writers* and *Deleted Names* (both from A Midsummer Night's Press) and one written in Spanish, *Desayuno en la cama* (Egales). In addition to his own writing, he is a prolific literary translator. Recent book translations into English include the poetry collections: *Nothing is Lost: Selected Poems by Jordi Doce* (Shearsman Books), *I'd ask you to join me by the Río Bravo to weep but you should know neither river nor tears remain* by Jorge Humberto Chávez (Shearsman Books), *Correspondences: An Anthology of Contemporary Spanish LGBT Poetry* (Egales), *Destruction of the Lover* by Luis Panini (Pleiades Press, 2019), Impure Acts by Ángelo Néstore (Indolent Books, 2019), and I Offer My Heart as a Target by Johanny Vazquez Paz (Akashic, 2019). Recent poetry book translations into Spanish include *Geografía del amor* by Kätlin Kaldmaa (Cuarto Propio), *La caligrafía de la aguja* by Arvis Viguls (Valparaíso), and *Amnesia colectiva* by Koleka Putuma (co-translated with Arrate Hidalgo, Flores Raras). He has lived in Madrid, Spain, since 1999.

The Cliff Becker Book Prize in Translation

"Translation is the medium through which American
readers gain greater access to the world. By provid-
ing us with as directa connection as possible to the
individual voice of the author,translation provides a
window into the heart of a culture."

—Cliff Becker, May 16, 2005

Cliff Becker (1964–2005) was the National Endowment for the Arts Liter-
ature Director from 1999 to 2005. He began his career at the NEA in 1992
as a literature specialist, was named Acting Director in 1997, and in 1999 be-
came the NEA's Director of Literature.

The publication of this book of translation is a reflection of Cliff's
passionate belief that the arts must be accessible to a wide audience and not
subject to vagaries of the marketplace. During his tenure at the NEA, he ex-
panded support for individual translators and led the development of the
NEA Literature Translation Initiative. His efforts did not stop at the work-
place, however. He carried his passion into the kitchen as well as into the
board room. Cliff could often be seen at home relaxing in his favorite,
wornout, blue T-shirt, which read, "Art Saves Me!" He truly lived by this
credo.

To ensure that others got the chance to have their lives impacted by un-
censored art, Cliff hoped to create a foundation to support the literary arts
which would not be subject to political changes or fluctuations in patronage,
but would be marked solely for the purpose of supporting artists, and in
particular, the creation and distribution of art which might not otherwise
be available. While he could not achieve this goal in his short life, seven years
after his untimely passing, his vision was realized.

The Cliff Becker Endowment for the Literary Arts was established by
his widow and daughter in 2012 to give an annual publication prize in trans-
lation in his memory. The Cliff Becker Book Prize in Translation annually
produces one volume of literary translation in English. It is our hope that
with ongoing donations to help grow the Becker Endowment for the Literary
Arts, important artists will continue to touch, and perhaps save, lives of
those whom they reach through the window of translation.

Donations to The Cliff Becker Endowment for the Literary Arts will help ensure that Cliff 's vision continues to enrich our literary heritage. It is more important than ever before that English-speaking readers are able to comprehend our world and our histories through the literatures of diverse cultures. Tax deductible donations to the Endowment will be gratefully received by White Pine Press. Checks should be made payable to White Pine Press and sent to The Cliff Becker Endowment for the Literary Arts, c/o White Pine Press, P.O. Box 236, Buffalo, NY 14201.

Cliff Becker Book Prize in Translation

Hatchet - Carmen Boullosa. Translated by Lawrence Schimel. 2020

Bleeding from All 5 Senses - Mario Santiago Papasquiaro. Translated by Cole Heinowitz. 2019

The Joyous Science: Selected Poems - Maxim Amelin. Translated by Derek Mong & Anne O. Fischer. 2018

Purifications or the Sign of Retaliation - Myriam Fraga. Translated by Chloe Hill. 2017

Returnings: Poems of Love & Distance - Rafael Alberti. Translated by Carolyn L. Tipton. 2016

The Milk Underground - Ronny Someck. Translated by Hana Inbar & Robert Manaster. 2015

Selected Poems of Mikhail Yeryomin. Translated by J. Kates. 2014

A Hand Full of Water - Tzveta Sofronieva. Translated by Chantel Wright. 2012